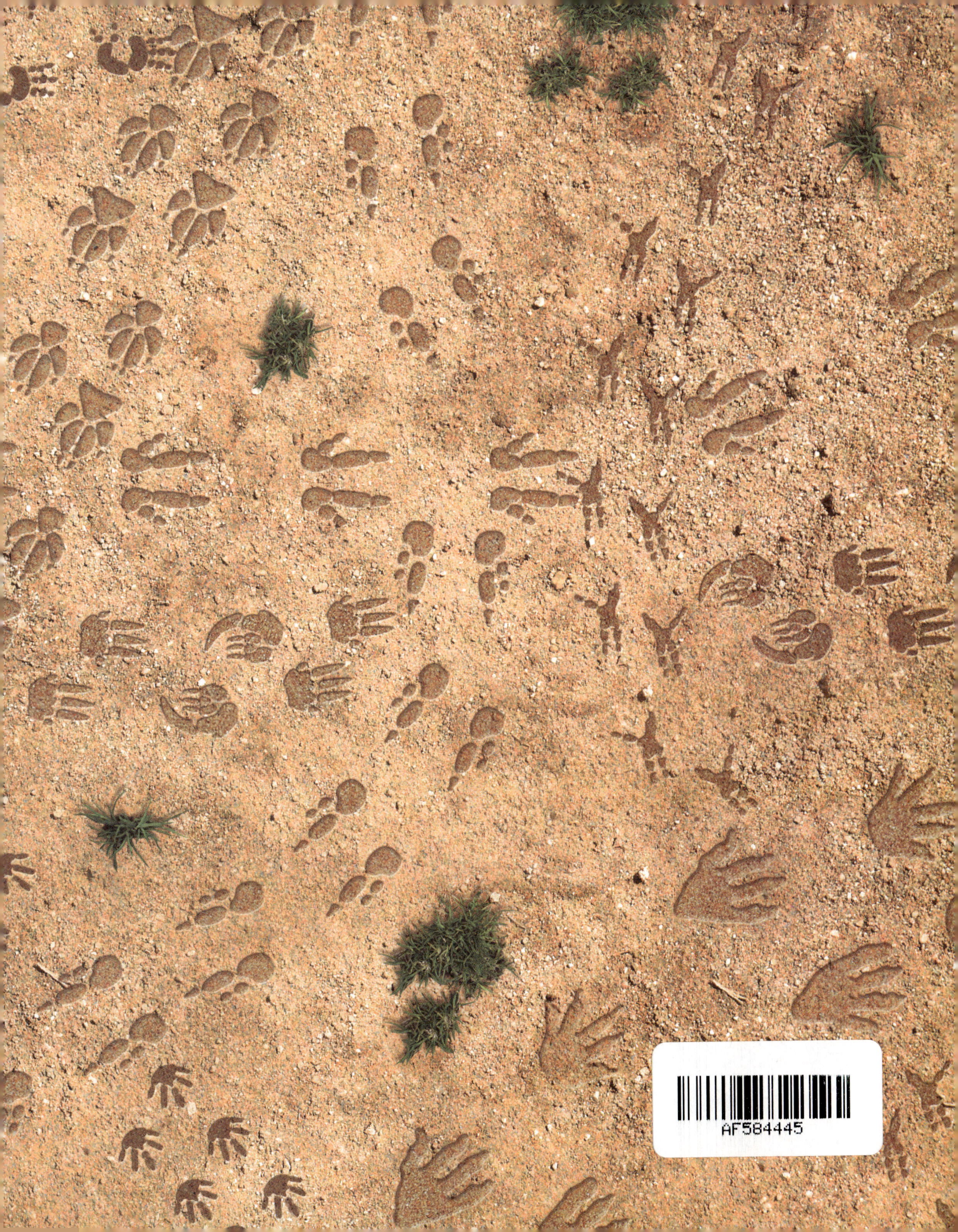

AF584445

AUSTRALIA'S REMARKABLE WILDLIFE

JOHN LESLEY

POSSUM

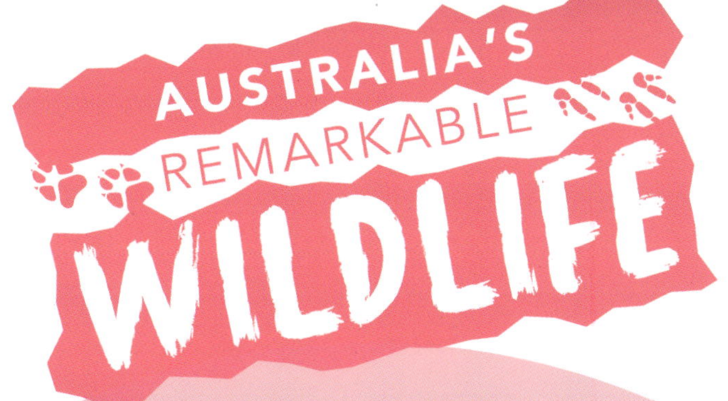

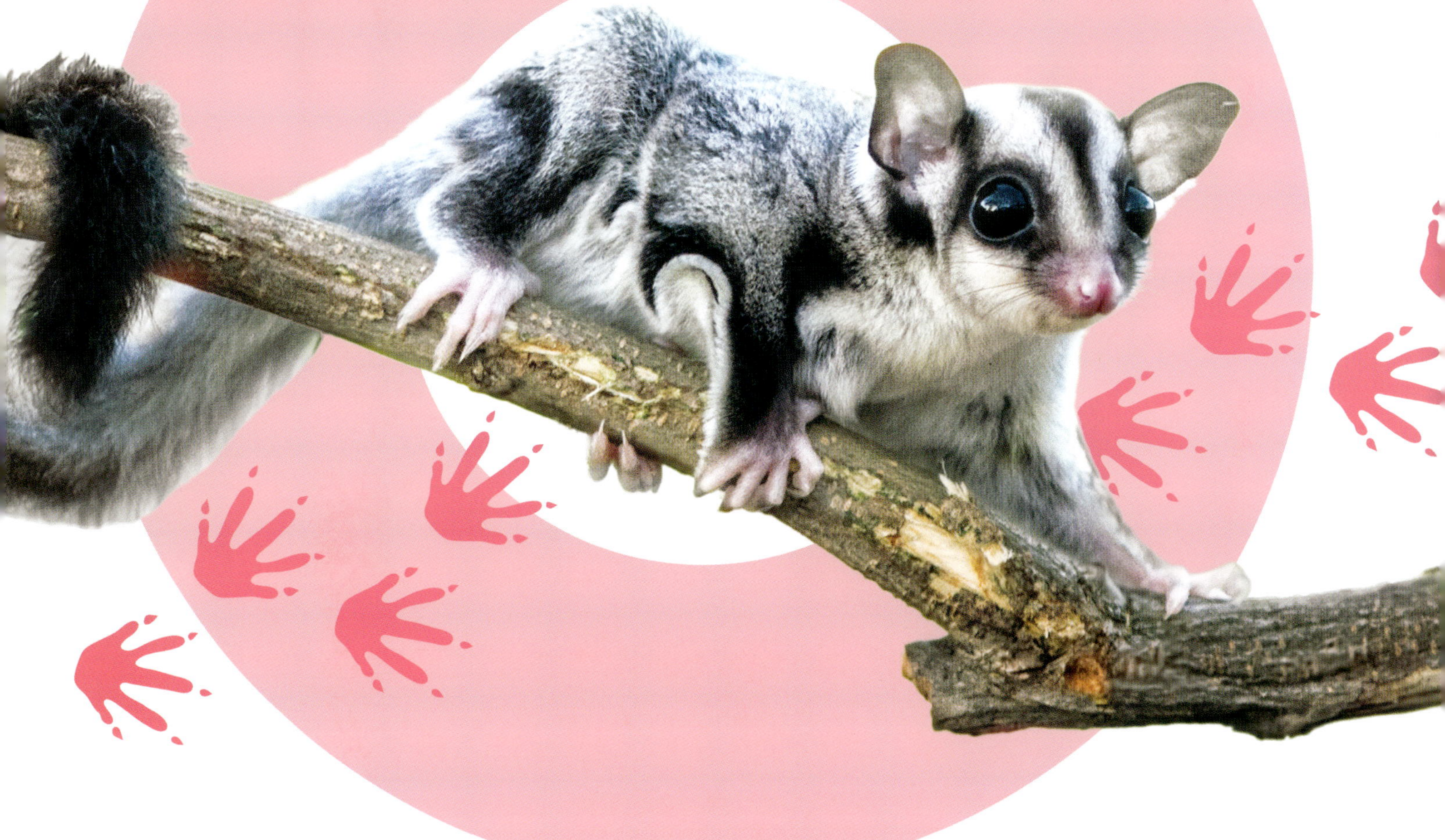

REDBACK publishing

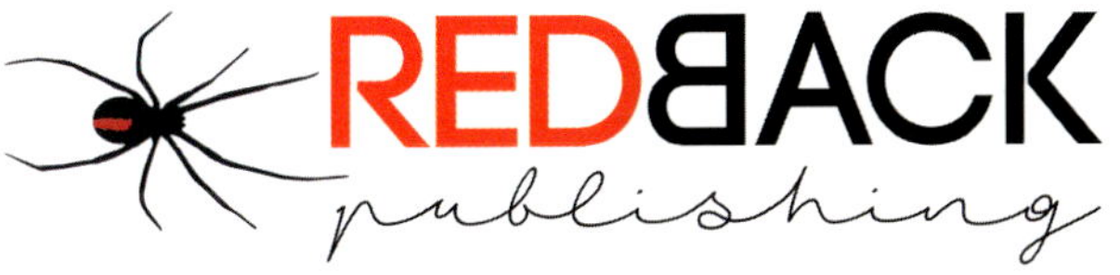

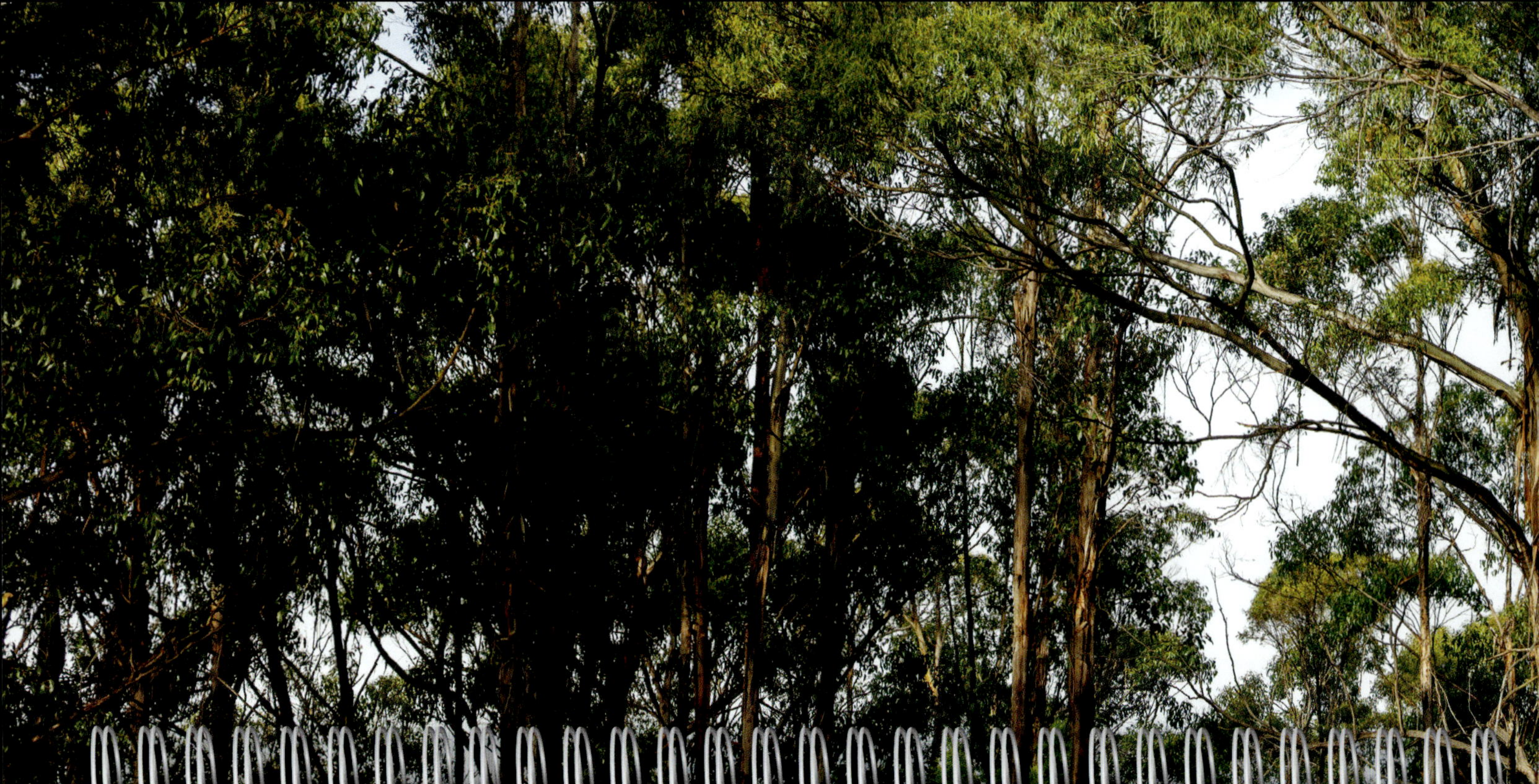

First Published 2025
Redback Publishing
Suite 6, 13a Narabang Way,
Belrose NSW 2085
Australia

www.redbackpublishing.com
orders@redbackpublishing.com

ISBN 978-1-761401-35-0

Author: John Lesley
Editors: Lucinda Dodds and Emma Dobinson
Design: Redback Publishing

A catalogue record for this book is available from the National Library of Australia

Acknowledgements
Abbreviations: l—left, r—right, b—bottom, t—top, c—centre, m—middle
We would like to thank the following for permission to reproduce photographs: (Images © shutterstock)

p14b G A Hoye © Australian Museum, p26b - lovemydesigns / Shutterstock.com, p28lt - Tirin (www.takver.com), CC BY-SA 3.0 <https://creativecommons.org/licenses/by-sa/3.0>, via Wikimedia Commons, p28rt - Samrhorton, CC BY-SA 4.0 <https://creativecommons.org/licenses/by-sa/4.0>, via Wikimedia Commons.

CONTENTS

WHAT IS A POSSUM?

What is that animal thumping around on the roof and leaving nasty, wet patches seeping through the ceiling? If you live in Australia, it's likely to be a possum.

Possums are loved and hated by homeowners, farmers and gardeners. These furry marsupials eat plants, flowers, insects and fruit, and some have adapted well to living near people and making use of all the food sources that humans create.

There are over 20 types of possum that are native to Australia. They range in size from tiny ones that are the size of a mouse, to bigger ones that can glide through the air, and others that are as large and heavy as a small dog.

Some possums are called gliders or cuscus.

PLAYING POSSUM

'Playing possum' is a term that means to pretend to be dead. This is what American opossums do to confuse an attacker. Australian possums don't do this.

MARSUPIALS

All possums are marsupials. The characteristics of a marsupial are:

They have fur

They give birth to tiny, underdeveloped babies

The young drink milk from their mother who keeps them in a pouch or a fold of her skin

Australia's marsupial possums are distantly related to those of America. All possums had the same ancestor millions of years ago but have separated into many different species since then.

OPOSSUMS

Opossums do not live in Australia. They are native to North, Central and South America. Just like their distant Australian cousins, American female opossums also have a pouch where they keep their babies.

ORIGIN OF THE NAME

The name opossum comes from a First Nations American language. When Europeans first saw the Australian possums, they used the same name for them but dropped the 'o' at the beginning.

POSSUM BASIC FACTS

FEATURES

Possums have large, forward facing eyes. This gives them good vision at night, when they are active. Their noses are bare and pink, and they have long whiskers around the mouth.

LEGS AND CLAWS

Possums that climb trees need strong claws and hind limbs for hanging onto branches and bushes as they search for food. Many possums have opposable thumbs that can help them to grasp food and branches.

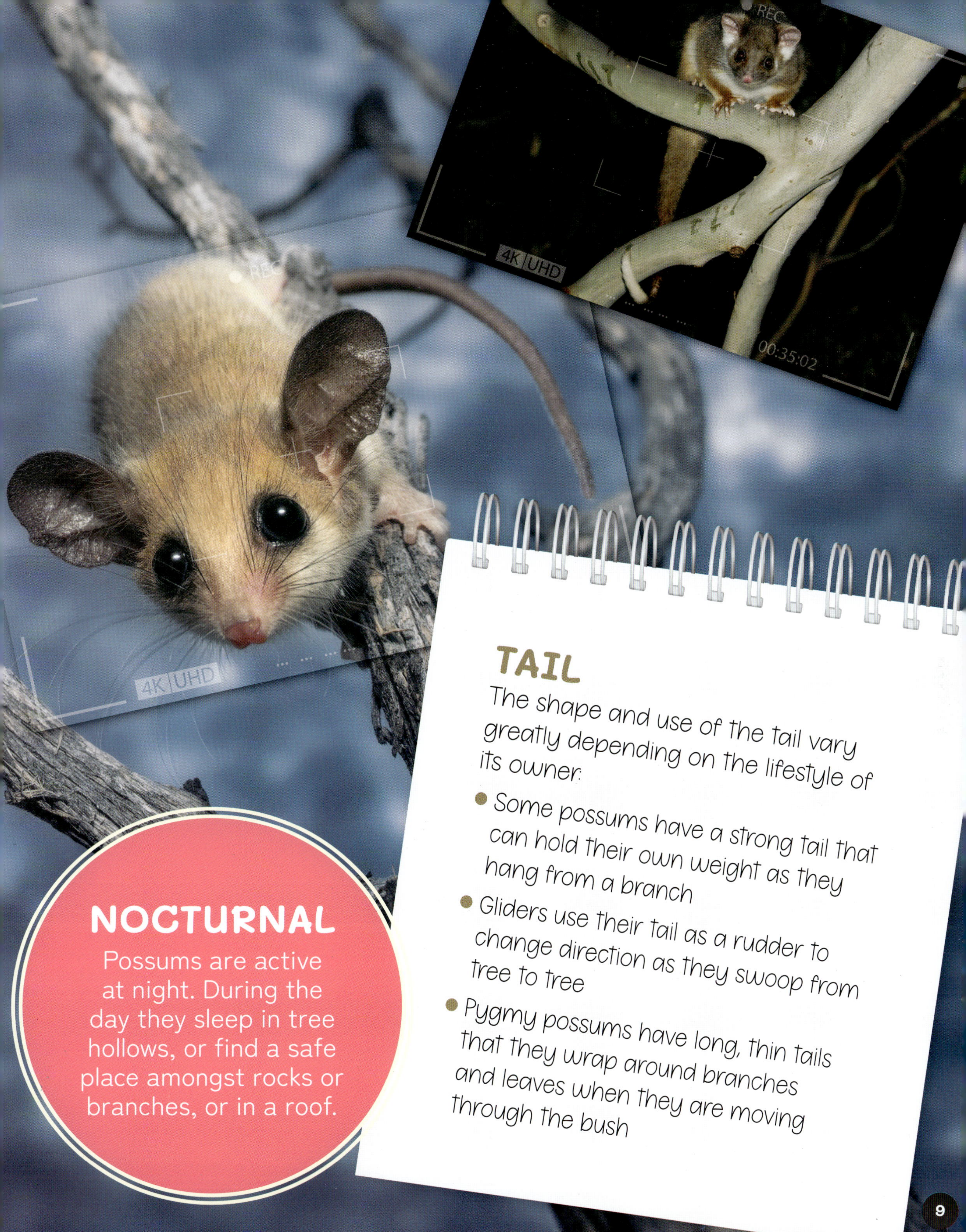

TAIL

The shape and use of the tail vary greatly depending on the lifestyle of its owner:

- Some possums have a strong tail that can hold their own weight as they hang from a branch
- Gliders use their tail as a rudder to change direction as they swoop from tree to tree
- Pygmy possums have long, thin tails that they wrap around branches and leaves when they are moving through the bush

NOCTURNAL

Possums are active at night. During the day they sleep in tree hollows, or find a safe place amongst rocks or branches, or in a roof.

TYPES OF POSSUMS

COMMON BRUSHTAIL POSSUM

THE BIGGEST!

The brushtails are the biggest and most numerous possums in Australia.

FACT FILE

- **Scientific name:** *Trichosurus vulpecula*
- **Colour:** Thick grey fur with a lighter colour on the belly. Tail ends in black fur
- **Size:** Size of a small dog. Weighs up to 4 kilograms. Tail about 40 centimetres long

- **Habitat:** Forests and wooded grasslands, as well as backyards with bushes and trees. They do not live in desert regions
- **Food:** Fruit, flowers and plants. Tame brushtails will eat anything offered, even if it is very unhealthy for them

When regularly fed by humans, these possums often become tame and may even come when called.

COMMON RINGTAIL POSSUM

FACT FILE

- **Scientific name:** *Pseudocheirus peregrinus*
- **Other name:** Eastern ringtail possum
- **Colour:** The fur is dark brown-grey on the back, and pale on the belly
- **Size:** Body about 30 centimetres long. The tail adds another 30 centimetres to the overall length. An adult weighs about 1 kilogram
- **Tail:** The tail has a white tip and is hairless on the underside, allowing it to be curled around a branch. This helps the possum hold on, leaving the other limbs free for finding food

LOOK, A RAT!

The ringtail possum is often mistaken for a large rat. You can tell the difference quickly by looking for the white tip on the possum's curling tail. Close-up, this lovely little possum is much more appealing than a rat.

- **Habitat**: Needs to live in trees and thick, tall bushes, including areas near where humans live. These possums do not usually like to live in roofs of houses. Ringtails live in forested areas in the eastern part of Australia
- **Nests**: If there are no tree hollows to hide in, ringtails gather sticks and leaves to make a safe nest in a tree
- **Food**: Plants, leaves and fruit

SMELL

Ringtails communicate mainly by smell. They rub their scent glands on branches so other ringtails will know they have been there.

DREY

A ringtail nest is called a drey, and it looks like a large, messy bird's nest.

MOUNTAIN PYGMY POSSUM

FACT FILE

- **Scientific name:** *Burramys parvus*
- **Colour:** Grey fur
- **Size:** About as big as a mouse
- **Habitat:** Rocky areas in alpine forests
- **Food:** Fruit, seeds and bogong moths

HIBERNATION

Mountain pygmy possums are the only Australian native animals that enter a deep sleep, called hibernation, during the winter. They live in the cold alpine regions of eastern Australia, where they build a burrow under the snow, and sleep there for up to four months during the winter.

Their continued survival is closely linked to the numbers of bogong moths which make up a large part of their diet. During the cold months, they feed on seeds that they have stored underground.

The mountain pygmy possum is now close to becoming extinct. This is due to loss of habitat, climate change, reduced food sources, and increased predation by feral animals such as cats and foxes. Sadly, it has no defences against any of these threats to its existence.

FUN FACT

- Mountain pygmy possums are tiny, beautiful and vulnerable to extinction
- They have tails that can grab branches as they move through bushes in search of food
- They are nocturnal and have large, bulging eyes and long whiskers to help them find their way around at night

HONEY POSSUM

The babies weigh a fraction of a gram.

FACT FILE

- **Scientific name:** *Tarsipes rostratus*
- **Other name:** Noolbenger
- **Colour:** Brown-grey fur with darker stripes down the back, and a pale belly
- **Size:** Less than 10 grams in weight, and only a few centimetres long, with a tail that is longer than the body
- **Habitat:** Southwest Australia, in bushland where there are many nectar-producing trees and bushes
- **Food:** Nectar and pollen

FUN FACT

Sometimes mistaken for a pygmy possum, the honey possum lives on nectar and pollen, like bees do. The honey possum has a long snout with a lot of whiskers at the tip. The tongue is long and thin, an adaptation for finding nectar in flowers. It stays in trees most of the time but will run across the ground if it has to.

The honey possum does not actually eat honey.

SUGAR GLIDER

FACT FILE

- Scientific name: *Petaurus breviceps*
- Colour: Thick grey fur, with a black stripe from the nose down to the tail, which is also tipped with black fur
- Size: Weighs about 150 grams and can be 30 centimetres long, including the tail
- Habitat: Forests of southeast Australia
- Food: Tree sap, pollen, nectar, insects and other small animals

Sugar gliders have a surprisingly long lifespan for such small animals, living up to ten years in the wild.

SUGAR GLIDER FACTS

The sugar glider can glide through the air by jumping from tree to tree and spreading out the flaps of skin between its limbs. It is a very skilled glider and can change direction during flight.

Sugar gliders are nocturnal. They have large eyes and perfect eyesight, adaptations necessary for gliding at night. They need tree hollows where they can sleep safely during the day. In very cold weather, they go into a deep sleep called torpor, which is much shorter than the sleep that hibernating animals experience.

They can glide for over 50 metres!

COMMON SPOTTED CUSCUS

FACT FILE

- **Scientific name:** *Spilocuscus maculatus*
- **Colour:** Soft, thick fur that is white with dark patches
- **Size:** The size of a pet cat. The long tail is curled at the tip and can grab branches
- **Habitat:** Lives in forests on Cape York, Queensland, and in New Guinea
- **Food:** Fruit, nectar, small animals and plants

People who see a cuscus often think it might be a monkey or a sloth, both of which do not exist in the wild in Australia.

The cuscus is a rare type of possum in Australia but it may be more numerous in the denser forests of New Guinea. Unlike its more southern relatives, it does not sleep in tree hollows, but in the forks of trees, much like a koala. The ears are small and hidden by thick fur.

The cuscus can be aggressive if it feels threatened and may hiss and scratch. They can live for about ten years in the wild.

POSSUM LIFE CYCLE

Possums are marsupials so they all give birth to tiny babies that look like embryos. Pygmy possum babies are the tiniest of all, measuring less than a centimetre. The babies crawl into the mother's pouch and stay there feeding on milk until they are big enough to leave. At this stage, they hang onto the fur on the mother's back, and she carries them around with her, teaching them what to eat and where to find food and water. In some possum species, the father helps to raise the young and may also carry them around on his back.

JOEYS AND PINKIES

Baby possums are called pinkies when they are born. When they grow a little larger in the pouch they are called joeys. This is the same name used for a baby kangaroo, which is also a marsupial.

LIFESPAN

The brushtail possums may live for over ten years. The large American opossum has a very short lifespan by comparison, living only about four years in the wild.

The smaller possums may only live a few years in the wild. A short lifespan is a factor that contributes to them being vulnerable to extinction, as they do not have as much opportunity as longer-lived possums to reproduce.

THREATS TO POSSUMS

IUCN RED LIST

The Red List is an international compilation of the conservation status of living things. Brushtail possums are very numerous and not under any threat of extinction. The pygmy possums and gliders are much more vulnerable, and some could become extinct in the future.

HABITAT LOSS

The main threat to all possums in Australia is the loss of forests, which provide a variety of native vegetation for food, and old trees with hollows for safety when sleeping.

CLIMATE CHANGE

The mountain pygmy possum is under threat from climate change as warmer winters disrupt its hibernation. It has evolved to wake at the same time as the bogong moths appear in masses. These are an important food source for it, but reduced numbers of bogong moths in recent years is having a negative effect on mountain pygmy possum numbers.

PROTECTING THEMSELVES

Large brushtail possums can bite and scratch and will fight if cornered. They also hiss and make a growling noise in an attempt to scare off a predator or a rival possum trying to enter their territory.

The pygmy possums and gliders have very few defences, which contributes to them being under threat if there is no safe habitat where they can hide.

PREDATORS

- Feral predators, as well as domestic dogs and cats, kill possums. Small possums are particularly vulnerable, but a big brushtail possum can fight off a cat or small dog
- Crows, currawongs and magpies will attempt to kill a small possum, or any baby possum they find
- Pythons will climb trees or enter roofs to find possums and kill them
- If a possum ends up in a territory that belongs to another possum, it can be injured or driven out

POSSUMS AND PEOPLE

DISEASES

If you are scratched or bitten by a possum, the wound can become infected. Possums in Australia are not aggressive, but they will defend themselves if you get too close.

ROADS

Dead possums on the side of the road are very common in country areas and the suburbs of cities all around Australia.

POSSUM TRAPS

Possums are protected wildlife in Australia, so they cannot be harmed. A licence is needed to trap possums for removal from a roof. A condition of this licence usually requires that the possum is released nearby so that it is not left in an area where it is confused and vulnerable to attack by predators or other possums.

Sealing up entry points into the roof of a house is the best way to stop possums causing a nuisance.

HUNTING

Although Australian brushtail possums are an introduced pest in New Zealand, and can be killed there, hunting possums in Australia is illegal.

MORE POSSUMS

Leadbeater's possum
Gymnobelideus leadbeateri

Greater glider
Petauroides Volans

Eastern pygmy possum
Cercartetus nanus

Feathertail glider
Acrobates pygmaeus

Tasmanian pygmy possum
Cercartetus lepidus
00:35:02
4K UHD
Squirrel glider
Petaurus norfolcensis
Yellow-bellied glider
Petaurus australis
4K UHD
3...2...1...1...2...3
00:35:02
Striped possum
Dactylopsila trivirgata
...2...3

SORTING ANIMALS INTO GROUPS

Biologists divide all living things around the world into groups. They call this process classification. The two basic groups of animals are called:

VERTEBRATES

Vertebrates have a backbone

INVERTEBRATES

Invertebrates do not have a backbone

Vertebrates are further divided into five groups called classes. Possums are marsupials and belong in the class called Mammalia, which is the same class that humans belong to.

GLOSSARY

adaptation change in the body or behaviour that makes an animal better able to survive

alpine referring to mountain regions that are cold and icy

drey nest made by a ringtail possum

embryo underdeveloped baby that is not yet born

joey baby marsupial

marsupial mammal group that produces underdeveloped babies that drink milk from the mother

nocturnal active at night

opposable thumbs thumbs that can be moved across to touch other fingers

pinkie newborn marsupial

rudder flat surface used to steer a plane or a boat

INDEX